# The Spirits of the Land- Faeries and the Soul of Britain

## John Kruse

London, 2022

# Contents

# Introduction

> "The green land's name that a charm encloses,
> It never was writ in the traveller's chart."[1]

What is it that attaches us to the land?  What gives us the sense of a spirit in the landscape, that the British countryside may be alive and preserves a body of memory and meaning for us?

My argument in this book is that, as spirits of the land, the faeries connect us directly and physically to Britain.  What's more, we are drawn to sites such as ancient prehistoric monuments precisely because they are symbols of this and to natural features such as springs because they are a tangible manifestation of a deeper psychic bond.  We feel close to Nature at a 'holy well' simply because of its immediate presence and our ability to interact intimately and freely.

The writer and researcher Sophia Kingshill, in describing the origins of Scottish legends and folklore, said this:

> "To personify the forces of nature is a way of understanding them and stories which explain the world help to give people (if only in imagination) some control over their surroundings and circumstances.  That is the essence of folklore… Although legends may not have been considered as literally true, they gave structure and guidance, bridging the gap between human beings and the invisible powers around them."[2]

This is, indeed, the folklorist explanation of our native myths and legends, hence Kingshill continues by doubting "how much anyone *believed* that still-birth or cot-death were caused by baby-snatching fairies, but… it is certain that straw crosses

---

[1] Algernon Charles Swinburne, *A Ballad of Dreamland.*
[2] S. Kingshill & J. Westwood, *The Lore of Scotland,* 2009, 'Introduction,' ix.

or steel pins were widely used as protection against the marauders…"

My approach has always been to accept that people in the past knew very well what they had experienced.  For centuries, individuals have described how they encountered and interacted with faeries. I have always chosen to believe them and to accept that they were neither liars nor deluded, nor imagining supernatural explanations for purely physical or physiological events.  Accordingly, I do not regard myself as writing folklore but faerylore.  This book proceeds on that basis.  For millennia the British have been aware of the Good Neighbours inhabiting these lands by their sides.  Here I try to understand the meaning of that parallel presence, developing some of the ideas first set out in my 2021 book *Faeries and the Natural World*.[3]

---

[3] Green Magic Publishing, 2021, chapter 4.

# A Sacred Landscape

The British landscape is freighted with the influences of millennia of legend-making and belief. The result can be that certain locations are charged with this accumulated spiritual meaning.  An example comes from the life of the composer John Ireland (1869-1972).

In 1933, Ireland was visiting the South Downs in Sussex. He was working on a new composition (what would become the piano concerto *Legend*) and he set out alone early one morning to walk up onto the top of the Downs between Arundel and Worthing so as to visit a ruined chapel called Friday's Church at Harrow Hill (see later as well).  What drew Ireland onto the Downs in the first place seems to have been a local tradition concerning the ghosts of children from a medieval leper colony that had once been situated west of Harrow Hill, at what is now the very remote Lee Farm.  Ireland seems to have been making something of a pilgrimage to the site, following an established route formerly used by the lepers and the priest who journeyed out to hold a weekly service for them. In addition to the dedicated chapel, the nearby churches of Clapham and Burpham have 'leper windows' which would have allowed the colony's inmates to witness masses held there.

Part of the reason that the chapel was constructed is that there was already a healing well or spring on the site.  It is still marked by a large pool and it has been speculated that 'Friday' may originally have been the Norse goddess 'Freya' and the 'church' may originally have denoted some barrows in the vicinity.  Harrow Hill itself is the site of a hillfort which itself is marked by the depressions of numerous Neolithic flint mines.  This whole area of the South Downs is covered by similar mines, as well as hillforts and burial mounds.

Arriving at the site that morning, Ireland was very irritated to find that he was not alone, despite the early hour.  A group of children dressed in white appeared near him and started dancing.  He watched them for some time before it began to dawn upon him that the infants themselves made no sound and that their feet upon the turf were silent.  He looked away, briefly distracted, and- when he turned back- they had vanished.

Ireland was convinced that he had had a faery experience (rather than seeing the ghosts of medieval lepers).  The incident definitely has all the hallmarks of an authentic faery contact: the individuals he saw were of child stature, they were engaged in dancing outdoors, yet were at the same time slightly detached from the material world, and, lastly, a moment's inattention broke the spell and allowed them to vanish.

The composer wrote in detail about this incident to his friend, the Welsh author Arthur Machen. Machen was convinced of the accrued ancient power of certain monuments and landscapes, as his famous book *The Hill of Dreams* captures so well.  His laconic reply to Ireland was: "Oh, so you've seen them too?"

This account reminds me strongly of one relayed by Sir Arthur Conan Doyle in his book, *The Coming of the Fairies* (1922). He had been told about a faery experience by a Mr. J. Foot Young, a well-known water diviner:

> "Some years ago, I was one of a party invited to spend the afternoon on the lovely slopes of Okeford Hill, in the county of Dorset. The absence of both trees and hedges in this locality enables one to see without obstruction for long distances. I was walking with my companion, who lives in the locality, some little distance from the main party, when to my astonishment I saw a number of what I thought to be very small children, about a score in number, and all dressed in little gaily-coloured short skirts, their legs being bare. Their hands were joined, and all held up, as they merrily danced round in a perfect

circle. We stood watching them, when in an instant they all vanished from our sight. My companion told me they were fairies, and that they often came to that particular part to hold their revels. It may be our presence disturbed them."[4]

Rather like the area of Sussex where Ireland was walking, Okeford Hill, near to the village of Child Okeford, is the site of an ancient earthwork and the whole scarp slope of the Downs thereabouts is marked with hillforts, barrows and prehistoric settlements.

Both these incidents or encounters took place in landscapes that had been occupied and venerated for many centuries. This may be because they had established faery links, or it could be that the faeries themselves may have been drawn to the pre-existing magic or sanctity of the locations.  Whatever the exact explanation, the fact is that they are present at these spots and are intermingled with centuries of human usage, belief and story-telling.  The land is sacralised through layers of meaning, of which the faeries are both symbols and participants.

---

[4] Sir Arthur Conan Doyle, *The Coming of the Fairies,* c.VII, 'Some Subsequent Cases.'

In his introductory note to the 1970 reprint of Alfred Watkins'
ley line classic, *The Old Straight Track,* John Michell noted
how both Watkins and the Reverend Francis Kilvert had
invoked the "same *genius terrae britannicae"* of the red
Herefordshire earth.  This *genius,* the 'spirit of the British land,'
is very much what we are describing when we discuss British
fairies.[5]

As has just been seen with John Ireland, artists and writers
have shown themselves to be peculiarly sensitive to this
spiritual aspect of the landscape.  What's more, faery lore has
had a profound influence upon the development of our culture,
inspiring poetry, painting, music and more.

## Paul Nash

The British painter Paul Nash (1889-1946) sought to discover
and free the imprisoned spirit, the motive power, that animated
the British landscape.  He deeply felt that a spirit of place, a
*genius loci,* inhabited the country's soil and scenery and that
certain poets in particular sensed it.  The visionary painter *and*
poet William Blake, Nash felt, "perceived, among many things,
the hidden significance of the land he always called Albion.
For him, Albion possessed great spiritual personality…  His
poetry literally came out of England…  Turner, again, sought
to break through the deceptive mirage… to a reality more
real…"  Nash, too, in his own work, sought to penetrate
beyond surface appearances; he explained that:

> "The landscapes I have in mind are no part of the unseen
> world in the psychic sense, nor are they part of the
> Unconscious. They belong to the world that lies visibly
> about us. They are unseen merely because they are not
> perceived."

---

[5] Alfred Watkins, *The Old Straight Track,* Abacus edition, 1970, xvii.

Nash was referring, here, to Maiden Castle and the Vale of the White Horse.  For him, the latter was a "landscape of terrific animation." Within such settings, he was interested in detecting what was "strange [and] poetical."[6]

Nash had first sensed the feeling that a place expressed "something more than its natural features seemed to contain" in the garden of his boyhood home at Iver Heath in Buckinghamshire.  Here he became aware of "something which the ancients spoke of as *genius loci*- the spirit of the place, but something that did not suggest that the place was haunted or inhabited by a genie in a psychic sense." Although the young painter here denied any supernatural character to these experiences or sensations, at other times he seemed more open to such an interpretation.[7]

Indeed, Nash could discover a 'place' with a unique and detectable atmosphere even in the most busy and unlikely of locations, such as Kensington Gardens in central London.  In his autobiography *Outlines,* which covers the earlier part of his life and career, the artist described playing there as a very young boy, "at a time before Barrie took over" (in other words, before Peter Pan became inseparably associated with the gardens).  Nash then observed: "The place was not infested by fairies; you found them in just one special place, if you wanted them."  It seems that the meaningful place that young Nash sensed was a spot that derived its uniqueness partly from the purely accidental arrangement of the trees and the resulting sense of secrecy, but also from a supernatural aura (but only *if* you were alive to it). This was a sensitivity to atmosphere- except that an observer actively contributed to that by the knowledge that he or she brought to the place.[8]

---

[6] Nash, 'Personal Statement,' *Unit One* (edited by Herbert Read), 1934; 'Unseen Landscapes' *Country Life*, May 1938, vol.83, no.2157, 526.
[7] Personal Statement, *Unit One,* 1934; Paul Nash, *Outline*, 1949, 106-7.
[8] Paul Nash, *Outline*, chapter 1.

In fact, the faeries seem never to have been too far from Nash's vision of the countryside- at least, early in his life. In 1913 he drew a picture of strip lynchets on the Berkshire Downs, which he called *Their Hill.* As it happened, the owner of the land saw the picture at an exhibition and asked Nash the reason for the title. He replied "I felt it was the sort of hill which could not belong to anyone in particular, but to an ancient people or to the fairies, even."[9]

## Home Counties Hamadryads

Intriguingly, Nash repeatedly drew analogies between human life and the lives of trees: he was keenly aware of how a tree was rooted in the soil and dependent upon the earth and landscape.  In a letter written in August 1912 the painter even went so far as to declare that he painted them as though they were human because "I sincerely love and worship trees and know that they are people- and wonderfully beautiful people." These ideas make his comments upon Ivinghoe Beacon, on the Chiltern Hills, even more fascinating and relevant: it was, he recalled, "an enchanted place... where you might meet anything from a polecat to a dryad." The woodland spirits were alive and active for Nash.[10]

So it was that, for Paul Nash, the hill top group of beech trees at Wittenham Clumps, near Wallingford in Berkshire, were a key part of a landscape that was "full of strange enchantment; on every hand it seemed a beautiful legendary county haunted by old gods long forgotten." The trees themselves fascinated him and he strove repeatedly to create "an image of them which could express what they meant to me… that would convey the strange character of the place… would contain the individual spirit."[11]

---

[9] Nash, *Outline,* 128.
[10] Letter to Gordon Bottomley, August 1st, 1912, in Abbott & Bertram, *Poet & Painter,* 1955, 42; letter to Audrey Withers, c.1924, Victoria & Albert Museum, no.14.
[11] Letter to Mercia Oakley, September 23rd 1911; Nash, *Outline,* 122.

Poet Herbert Read described Paul Nash as a painter "dedicated to the *genius loci.*"  He experienced "profound intuitions" that enabled him, through his art, to "reveal the immemorial values in the landscape." He saw "an animistic landscape, the sacred habitation of familiar spirits" in which many natural elements- the shell, the withered stalk, the flower and leaf, the fungus, tree and cloud- were magically synthesised through what Read termed a "druidic ritual."[12]

Through his strong sense of the character and spirit of individual places, Nash felt that he could witness "another aspect of the accepted world..." In this, he saw himself merely to be continuing a tradition that had been initiated by Wordsworth, who had built up a mythology founded upon a "systematic animation of the inanimate, which attributes life and feeling to non-human nature."[13]

Elsewhere, Nash wrote that "The idea of giving life to inanimate objects is as old as almost any record of fable.  It has varied in its conception throughout very different histories," which included fairy lore and mythology.  This "endowment of natural objects, organic but not human, with active powers or personal influences" lies at the core of faery belief, I also believe.  The artist wrote these lines having recently visited the Avebury stone circle for the first time; it had evidently impressed him deeply.  He continued that "it is not a question of a particular stone being the house of the spirit- the stone itself has its spirit; it is alive." This idea of animating inanimate objects was very old indeed, "a commonplace in fairy tale and which occurs quite naturally also in most mythologies."[14]

---

[12] Read, *Paul Nash,* Penguin Modern Painters, 1944, 14-15.
[13] Nash, 'The Life of the Inanimate Object,' *Country Life,* May 1st 1937.
[14] Nash, 'The Life of the Inanimate Object,' *Country Life,* May 1st 1937.

Sketching at Silbury Hill near Avebury, Nash recalled that:

> "I felt that I had divined the secret of that paradoxical pyramid.  Such things do happen in England, quite naturally, but they are not recognised for what they are- the true yield of the land, indeed, but also works of art; identical with the intimate spirit inhabiting these gentle fields, yet not the work of chance or the elements, but directed by an intelligent purpose ruled by an authentic vision."[15]

Nash's revelation at Silbury encouraged him to intensify his search for a "character which frankly disclosed a national inspiration, something whose lineaments seemed almost redolent of place and time within the limits of these shores."

As already noted, Nash was especially devoted to the twin Oxfordshire hills called the Wittenham Clumps, which he returned to paint throughout his life.  It wasn't just the striking trees on the skyline that attracted and intrigued him.  The legends attached to the Clumps enhanced their mystery: one of the hills was an ancient fort where it was said that treasure was buried, guarded by a phantom raven.  On the plain beneath the hills were long barrows and the remnants of an ancient forest.  The place had, he said, "a compelling magic."[16]

As we've just seen as well, Nash discussed the spirits as the 'yield' of the land. Earlier investigators at Avebury had (incredibly) dismissed the stone circle and avenues as purely natural features, but he rightly saw them as more than a simple geological formation.  Elsewhere the painter discussed how his art would become preoccupied with "one landscape [and the] flowers and fungi which it yields."[17]  This suggests

---

[15] 'A Characteristic,' *Architectural Record*, March, 1937, 39-40.
[16] Nash's description of his painting, *Landscape of the Vernal Equinox,* 1944.

that, almost like crops or the native fauna and flora, the faery folk are a natural outgrowth of the soil.  The concept of 'yield' has an agrarian origin and it is indeed easy to imagine that our predecessors might have understood this in almost literal sense.  The commonest colour of faery clothing is green, the colour of vegetation, and if this idea were to be combined with an awareness of them living beneath the earth surface and emerging into our world from there, an image of the faeries springing like plants from our native soil would readily present itself.

I think we could usefully borrow a further term from English property law and talk about the 'burden' of the land: this is a term denoting certain costs or obligations that come with a certain body of real estate.  In faery terms, these will be the ancient right and expectation to be given a share of food products, to be able to use the occupiers' homes and other buildings and (even) to have certain areas of land set aside and preserved solely for them. They are a continual presence on the land- and a continual influence upon its usage and meaning.

Over and above his writings, of course, Nash created memorable images of the ancient British landscape.  Amongst these are *The Landscape of the Megaliths* (1934 and 1937), *Equivalents of the Megaliths* (1935) and *Circle of Monoliths* (1937), which all refer to Avebury, and *Nocturnal Landscape* (1938), which depicts Men an Tol in Penwith.  The art historian Sam Smiles has said of these images that Nash "evoked the uncanny."  The megaliths he depicted "have an almost animate presence… [they exist] in dream-like scenes where real topography is compressed and distorted in an environment dominated by their insistent otherness."[18]

---

[17] Letter to Dudley Tooth, May 1943.
[18] Smiles, *British Art- Ancient Landscapes,* 2017, 90.

Very often the British faeries seem very clearly to function as *genii loci*- spirits of place.  In one account, for example, they almost seem to be so intimately associated with a location that they are part of the fabric of a building itself.  On the Scottish island of Tiree, there was once a house that was plagued by faeries.  They used to sit on the rafters in swarms and they would sometimes drop down and steal a potato from the pot over the fire.  Eventually, the tenant decided to move away.  He built a new home some distance away but, unluckily, ran out of materials before he'd finished.  He took a stone from the old house to complete the job- which meant that the nuisance faeries he'd being trying to escape came along too.

Fascinatingly, in this connection, Fortescue Hitchins and Samuel Drew, in their 1824 opus on *The History of Cornwall*, had this to say of faery belief in the county.  They felt that the faery faith was fading, except amongst the aged and 'unenlightened' (by which they meant ignorant), but still:

> "By some, even the places of their resort are still pointed out, and particular fields and lanes are distinguished as spots which they were accustomed to frequent.  To these bushes and hedges, near which they were presumed to assemble, some degrees of veneration are still attached.  An indefinite species of sanctity is still associated with their beaten circles [that is, the fairy rings where they danced] and it is thought unlucky to injure their haunts or throw any obstacle in their way."[19]

Hitchins and Drew noted too that William Borlase, in his 1769 book on *The Antiquities of Cornwall*, had also observed how the Cornish still saw the spriggans and pixies as real beings having power over the weather and the affairs of men and, as such, deserving of respect: "these inferior deities… answer to

---

[19] Hitchins & Drew, *The History of Cornwall,* 1824, vol.1, 97.

the *genii* and fairies of the ancients… and they pay them a kind of veneration."[20]  In other words, certain spots were treated almost as shrines because the pixies were linked so powerfully with them.  As I have already speculated, they may therefore be viewed as being a part of the land itself.

A Land

Paul Nash was, by no means, the only artist or author to be attuned to the spirits of the land.  The earlier British writer Maurice Hewlett had had the same perceptions as Nash.  In his 1913 novella *The Lore of Proserpine,* he recorded how "I have seen spirits, beings… and have observed them as part of the landscape, no more extraordinary than grazing cattle or wheeling plover."  A little later in the same book, he added that he regarded them as a "natural fact… a part of the landscape."[21]

In the 1930s the painter John Piper became friendly with archaeologist Stuart Piggott, who had helped restore the Avebury stone circle, and for a while the pair planned a joint project, a book that sought to make archaeology accessible to the public, partly through Piper's illustrations.  The plan was that it would stress "the importance of the field monuments as a part of the English scene and an important feature in the landscape."  The idea never came to fruition, but it could have been an interesting expression of the unity of science, culture and emotion, combining archaeology and the motivating power of myth.  Elsewhere, John Piper described how Paul Nash was "identifying all nature with a Bronze Age standing stone"- a phrase suggestive of the deep resonance that these monuments can hold.[22]

---

[20] Borlase, *Antiquities of Cornwall,* 110.
[21] 'The Soul at the Window,' *The Lore of Proserpine*, 1913.
[22] Letter from Piggott to his wife, July 1st 1941, Piggott Correspondence at Oxford Institute of Archaeology; Piper, 'Lost: A Valuable Object,' in M. Evans, *The Painter's Object,* 1937, 70.

Perhaps archaeologist Jacquetta Hawkes' 1951 book, *A Land,* achieved something of what Piper and Piggott had envisaged. She explained in her preface that she had set out to evoke "the land of Britain, in which past and present, nature, man and art, all appear in one piece… I see a land as much affected by the creations of poets and painters as by changes of climate and vegetation."

Later, Hawkes alluded to very locally rooted poets, such as Thomas Hardy and John Clare, in whose verse "the images rising from the darkness of unconscious memory seem to be as much a part of the growth of that countryside as the distinctive plants and animals which it more directly supports." Their works were, therefore, a 'yield of the land.' As for the ancient megalithic tombs and circles, she appreciated their potency as symbols of rebirth and fecundity, without being able to determine which exactly their builders "honoured, the Great Mother or the Sky God, the local divinities or the spirits of their ancestors, and also the stones associated with them."[23]

In Cornwall the sculptor Barbara Hepworth was another artist sensitive to the power of the past. She described the county as "very fertile," which was not an agrarian assessment but a reference to the ability of its "pagan landscape" to inspire and excite the creative imagination. Hepworth was interested in the relationship of human beings to their landscape and saw this somehow echoed or symbolised by the megaliths: "any stone standing in the hills here is a figure." She even went so far as to declare "There is no landscape without the human figure: it is impossible for me to contemplate pre-history in the abstract. Without the relationship of man and his land, the mental image becomes a nightmare." Key to Hepworth's enquiries, then, were those prehistoric monuments- "incredible stones everywhere, so persistent and such an early civilisation…" The sense of connection to the deep past was clearly of considerable importance to her. Rather like Paul Nash, too, she tended to animate the land around her:

---

[23] Hawkes, 'Preface' to *A Land,* 1951.

"Landscape is strong- it has bones and flesh and skin and hair. It has age and history and a principle behind its evolution."[24]

Ithell Colquhoun

Also active in the same county at the same time as Barbara Hepworth was the surrealist and occultist Ithell Colquhoun. Colquhoun was preoccupied with magic throughout her life. For her, it was a constant reality- in her daily activities, in her dreams and expressed through her art. The artist saw dreams as a medium through which she could communicate with spirits and receive occult revelations.  These, in turn, could act as a source of inspiration for her art.

Colquhoun saw the cosmos as interdependent and interconnected, with each element effecting others. Hence, she said of Cornwall, in her 1957 book *The Living Stones,* that:

> "The life of a region depends ultimately on its geologic substratum, for this sets up a chain reaction which passes, determining their character, in turn through its streams and wells, its vegetation and the animal life that feeds on this, and finally through the type of human attracted to live there. In a profound sense also the structure of its rocks gives rise to the psychic life of the land: granite, serpentine, slate, sandstone, limestone, chalk and the rest each have their special personality, dependant on the age in which they were laid down, each being co-existent with a special phase of the earth-spirit's manifestation."[25]

---

[24] Letter to John Summerson, dated January 3rd 1940, in S. Festing, *Barbara Hepworth- A Life of Forms,* 1995, 141, 236, 99 & 15; Hepworth, *Barbara Hepworth: Carvings & Drawings,* 1952, c.4; A. Bowness, *Barbara Hepworth- Drawings from a Sculptor's Landscape,* 1966, 13.
[25] Quotations are from the 2016 edition of *The Living Stones,* 57.

During her long life, Colquhoun was initiated into a number of occult societies, such as Alistair Crowley's Ordo Templi Orientis, the Temple of Isis and the British Druid Order.  She regularly performed her own magical rituals and ceremonies. Her mystical practice was based upon Kabbalah, but she combined these teachings with the precepts of her Christian upbringing, as well as Tantra, meditation, earth magic, Celtic lore, Druidism and Wicca. Her researches included the Celtic gods, druidical ceremonies and tree lore.  Colquhoun's husband, Bill Picard, believed that she could see faeries and, very significantly, the artist was a member of the Fairy Investigation Society.

Colquhoun first moved to Cornwall to escape the Blitz during the Second World War.  In part, what drew her was the supernatural atmosphere that she sensed in the county.  She had detected "weirdness in the hidden corners" and found the county "enchanted… There is always something new to find in it- hidden well or ancient stone."  It was a place that could only be truly comprehended by walking through it, she maintained, "for this countryside, unlike some, is by no means passive but gives to the willing recipient and, in its turns, receives from those whom it has called to it, and a rhythmic interchange is established."[26]

The artist found a place to live at the head of the Lamorna valley, which was an established artistic colony.  Having chosen her new home, she addressed herself to the local spirits of the place:

> "Influences, essences, presences, whatever is here- in my name of a stream of in a valley I salute you; I share this place with you… Oh, rooted here without time I bathe in you; genius of the fern-loved gulley, do not molest me and may you remain forever unmolested."

---

[26] *Living Stones,* 129, 33 & 102.

For her, the valley possessed a weirdness, a strange atmosphere, and the artist readily accepted that, at night, "I am no longer mistress in my house, for another life will fill it until dawn."  She continued:

> "There are people who have felt in this valley that nature-spirits were weeping; imprisoned and misused by Druidism in decay…these spirits can only mourn.  Their life is not that of humanity- they are a separate race; the 'cream-bowl duly set' would not console them as it might the drudging goblin or lubber fiend who is nearer to human consciousness.  What can one do but offer them peaceful co-existence?"

In her reference to Milton's *L'Allegro,* Colquhoun deliberately distinguished the faery beings she sensed around her from the more domestic brownies and hobgoblins of English tradition; she was sharing her home with some wilder spirits.[27]

Her particular focus was the folklore associated with the standing stones and other ancient monument of the west of Cornwall, which she integrated with her own esoteric researches.  Colquhoun's book is full of folk tales of hags and of supernatural presences around thorn bushes and houses.  She was constantly alert to contacts with faery.  She heard faery music around Lamorna, as did others, and also related how the Helston Furry Dance was said to be an imitation of a faery dance once witnessed.[28]

She saw the ancient monuments of the region as living objects, endowed with mystical energies.  They had once been the scene of stone-worshipping rites and they continued to "emanate the residue of a powerful radiation," being "repositories still of ancient power" and imbued with psychic forces.  Colquhoun believed that the stones set up around ancient wells had absorbed the virtue of the springs they

---

[27] *Living Stones,* 22 & 53-54.
[28] *Living Stones,* 99 & 106.

guarded- or were holy rocks already before being incorporated into the shrine.  For her, the living stones of Penwith, danced, played music and ate just like people (or faeries) and they held "the secret of the country's inner life."[29]

Colquhoun was especially taken with the holy wells of Cornwall, such as that at Carn Euny, where she was aware of the rather neglected St Uny, the *genius loci*, "a nymph of wells and springs, whose retired presence only reveals itself now, perhaps, in some special condition of light and air, some mood of weather conjoined with locality."  The saint's strange, unused powers hovered about the place, a pervasive semi-human entity that the artist expressed through her ink drawing *Interior Landscape* (1947), showing the mystic connections between the chapel, the well and pitchers of water.

Around the same time, Colquhoun developed a fascination with the legend of St Warna, who has a healing well on the island of St Agnes in the Scillies.  This interest led to two series of pictures, *St Warna* and *Linked Islands,* in 1947, and to a number of prose poems on the saint's legend which were published in *The Glass* the following year.  The saint sailed to the Scillies from Ireland in a coracle and, having landed, the artist imagined her being absorbed into the landscape-becoming part of its spirit of place: "The process of her subsuming begins; her personal presence is from henceforth unseen, though acknowledged in every blade and pebble."  As for the saint's well, it works almost as an extension of this, bringing "all desires to fruit… Water fresh with suspension of unseen qualities, agents of wonder work. Life of crystal, life of sap and xylem, bast, bone, sinew and blood! Quick of the island, a sweet spray."[30]

*Genius Loci* (1946) is a painting of a pond on Hampstead Heath; the central motif of which, a grove of trees surrounding

---

[29] *The Living Stones,* 58-59 & 64.
[30] *Living Stones,* 67-71- see too 158 & chapter 'Germoe's Wells;' *The Glass,* 1948, 'Santa Warna Lands' & 'Santa Warna's Wishing Well.'

a pool of water, carried obvious pagan associations for Colquhoun, whilst the title of the picture confirms her wider awareness of presence of the tutelary deities around springs and ponds. Her *Dance of the Nine Opals* was based on the Merry Maidens stone circle, inland from her Lamorna home, which she associated with a solar festival or fertility rite. The painting, though, incorporates complex imagery from the kabbalah and alchemy. Her *Dance of the Nine Maidens* (1940) incorporated female figures within the same menhirs, as was the case too with *Sunset Birth* (1942), which shows the Men-an-Tol, combining its traditional use in curing infertility with the Indian concepts of *chakras* and *nadis*. Colquhoun's *Landscape with Antiquities (Lamorna)* of 1955 is an aerial view of all the major monuments in the vicinity of her home, connecting them with those routeways that she felt it so important to walk. She had written in *The Living Stones* how "One could make a map with patches of colour to mark the praeternatural character of certain localities, but these would intensify rather than vary the general hue. So, it is not surprising to find eerie places beyond the confines of Lamorna."[31]

As described, these "acknowledged relics of an unimagined age" were holy rocks, anciently magnetised and, for Colquhoun, full of psychic life, allowing "praeternatural contact that later orthodoxies have lost or been denied." Sensitive people could still detect these forces, "what folk tales have known for ages past, though now shut out of consciousness by a 'closed rationalism'."[32]

Conclusion

During the twentieth century, a number of British artists showed themselves responsive to the spirits of place within the country's landscapes. Whether this sensitivity arose from

---

[31] *The Living Stones,* 55.
[32] *Living Stones,* 58-59 & 99.

their creative natures, or whether it reflected the fact that- as painters- they were more likely to take time to study and to absorb their surroundings, is less clear. What they detected found expression through the medium of their works, but in essence their response was no different to the traditional stories and names that people had applied to the places around them for millennia.

The artists discussed all responded to spirits of place.  I feel that the British faeries are, indeed, the *genii loci* of the land; they are, in many respects, bound up with and directly expressive of the landscape within which they live.  Pixies, the *tylwyth teg*, the 'yarthkins' of East Anglian, are all a part of the terrain in which they reside; they are the animating spirit of those moors, mountains and fens.  The wild and aggressive spriggans, buccas and piskies of the south-west arguably manifest the rugged nature of the region they inhabit; so too the tiddy ones or yarthkins of the Fens, rising as they do from the waterways and peaty soils of that region.  They are the original and most fundamental yield of the land.

I need hardly say that these ideas are not by any means uniquely mine.  Well known faery artist Brian Froud, for example, has said that "Faeries are the inner nature of each land and a reflection of the inner nature of our souls."  The people of each nation are shaped by their environment; so too are the supernatural beings of that country and, as a result, there is a continual circular interaction between them all.

# Continuity

Part of the enduring spirit of the land is our own connection to it.  The British are part of Britain because they have been linked to it physically and emotionally for thousands of years.

## Language

Generation upon generation of people have lived upon the land and our roots go deep.  Before English, before the British Celtic (Brythonic) that produced Welsh and Cornish, people were present here speaking related languages.  It used to be thought that, before the Iron Age Celts settled in these lands, the inhabitants spoke some entirely different tongue; more or less plausible suggestions have included Phoenician, Berber, Basque and the language family that includes Etruscan.

The belief now is that, whilst the ancient British didn't speak a Celtic or Germanic language, they still spoke a language from the same broad family- Indo-European.  This group of tongues already covers a vast area, from Hindi and Urdu in India through Persian, Kurdish, the Slavic languages, Greek, the Latin and Germanic families to Celtic tongues such as Breton and Gaelic.  For pre-Celtic speech to be related is therefore not surprising.  This ancient, lost, language is often called 'Old European,' implying that- before about 1500BC- it was once spoken far more widely.[33]

The Old European of Britain has left traces in names for natural features, especially water courses.  The names of important rivers are very durable and the words often relate to those rivers' shape or qualities.  Well-known examples include Thames, meaning a dark river, Taw and Tay- perhaps the silent or powerful river, Stour- powerful, and Tees- boiling or surging.  Some river names, though, are very hard to interpret-

---

[33] See, for instance, Nicolaisen, *Scottish Place Names,* c.9, 'Pre-Celtic Names.'

for example, Severn and Colne- and there is some indication that a few of these will predate even Old European, being very ancient pre-Indo-European words.

Familiar names have therefore been passed on for generation after generation over huge periods of time.  In their continuity, they preserve some of the earliest impressions of, and reactions to, the land of Britain, as experienced by some of the very earliest Mesolithic settlers.

## Faery Speech

Here, it is worthwhile asking ourselves- what language do the faeries speak?  They can certainly converse with their current mortal neighbours; they have picked up enough English, Welsh, Gaelic and Manx to be able to interact perfectly effectively with the human populations around them, but this doesn't necessarily imply that this is how they might discuss matters amongst themselves.

There is definitely evidence to indicate that the faeries speak another language entirely- their own.[34]  Thus, a man called Thomas Edmund William, from Hafodafel, near Blaenau Gwent in South Wales, met a fairy procession and "heard them talking together in a noisy, jabbering way; but no-one could distinguish the words."  Other witnesses from Wales state the same: "they did not understand a word that was said; not a syllable did they comprehend…" whilst in another couple of encounters we are assured "it was not Welsh and she did not think it was English" that the *tylwyth teg* spoke.[35]

Very similar reports to the Welsh ones come from the Isle of Man.  Several Manx witnesses have stated that the 'little

---

[34] O. Swire, *Skye- The Island & Its Legends*, 7.  I have discussed faery language in several other books: see my *British Fairies,* 2017, c.3, *Faery,* 2020, c.4 & *Manx Faeries,* 2021.
[35] Wirt Sikes, *British Goblins*, 106; John Rhys, *Celtic Folklore,* 272, 277 & 279.

people' speak "a foreign tongue."  They may often be overheard talking together at night, but they cannot be understood.  In fact, the incomprehensibility of faery speech has been stressed repeatedly by witnesses on the island.[36]

This has led people to speculate on their origins.  Manx folklore expert Charles Roeder reported the following local theory about the faeries' speech:

> "There is no-one hearing them but the woman in the little shop.  She heard them at midnight one winter night in an elder tree, speaking a language she couldn't understand.  As she drew near, they whispered in her ear- but she couldn't understand.  Perhaps they were foreign fairies, visiting the Isle of Man, for in old tales the fairies speak Manx.  The Manx fairies have gone, or they have changed their language- like the people. Perhaps the fairies couldn't understand English so they changed their language out of spite: they can be spiteful when offended."[37]

Lastly, the faeries' language is no more recognisable in Scotland that it is further south.  A little grey trow woman was once seen on Shetland, trapped above ground by the daylight, and speaking to herself in an unknown tongue.  A changeling child seen in the north-east of Scotland during the eighteenth century was described to a folklorist by an old woman as being tiny, hairy creature which "gabbled and spak a lingo that naebody could understand and drew symbols in the ash that none could read."  This report makes very clear the fact that the faery folk have not only their own speech, but their own script as well.[38]

---

[36] See for example, *Manx Notes & Queries,* 1904, 118 & 129; *Yn Lioar Manninagh,* vol.III.

[37] Charles Roeder, *Skeealyn Cheeil Chiolee* (Manx Folk Tales), 1-2.

[38] Edmondson & Saxby, *The Home of a Naturalist,* 1888, 208; Milne, *Myths & Superstitions of the Buchan District,* 1891, 18.

Clearly there can be a language barrier between mortals and supernaturals, although the cause of that is uncertain.  Still, whilst there have unquestionably been changes in human speech as the result of colonisation and displacement, there's less reason for supposing that the same has happened amongst the faery folk. They seem much more permanent and constant, across the entirety of the British Isles.

We might, therefore, profitably revert to one of the oldest reports on this subject.  The cleric and writer, Gerald of Wales (1146-1223) travelled around Wales in 1188 with the Archbishop of Canterbury, recruiting for the forthcoming Third Crusade.  During that journey, he encountered a priest called Elidyr who told a very strange tale of his youth.  As a boy, he had entered faeryland and had spent considerable time there. He was able to give a great deal of information about their lifestyle, culture- and speech:

> "He had made himself acquainted with the language of that nation, the words of which, in his younger days, he used to recite, which, as the bishop often had informed me, were very conformable to the Greek idiom. When they asked for water, they said '*Ydor ydorum*,' which meant bring water, for *ydor* in their language, as well as in the Greek, signifies water, from whence vessels for water are called *ydrie*; and *dwr* also, in the British language, signifies water. When they wanted salt they said, '*Halgein ydorum*,' 'bring salt': salt is called *als* in Greek, and *halen* in British, for that language, from the length of time which the Britons (then called Trojans, and afterwards Britons, from Brito, their leader) remained in Greece after the destruction of Troy, became, in many instances, similar to the Greek.
>
> It is remarkable that so many languages should correspond in one word, *als* in Greek, *halen* in British, and *halgein* in the Irish tongue, the G being inserted; *sal* in Latin, because, as [the Latin grammarian] Priscian says, 'the S is placed in some words instead of an

aspirate, as *als* in Greek is called *sal* in Latin (*emi*–
semi, *epta*– septem), *sel* in French (the A being changed
into E), salt in English, by the addition of T to the
Latin; *sout*, in the Teutonic language: there are therefore
seven or eight languages agreeing in this one word.

If a scrupulous inquirer should ask my opinion of the
relation here inserted, I answer with Augustine, 'that the
divine miracles are to be admired, not discussed.' Nor do
I, by denial, place bounds to the divine power, nor, by
assent, insolently extend what cannot be extended. But I
always call to mind the saying of St. Jerome: 'You will
find,' says he, 'many things incredible and improbable,
which nevertheless are true; for nature cannot in any
respect prevail against the lord of nature.' These things,
therefore, and similar contingencies, I should place,
according to the opinion of Augustine, among those
particulars which are neither to be affirmed, nor too
positively denied."[39]

Gerald was too educated and rational a man to wholly accept
Elidyr's account, but as a faithful Christian he was loath to
reject it outright either.  What are we to make of it today,
though?  The adult Elidyr was a priest and plainly had
received an education that would have made him familiar with
Greek and Latin, giving him the elements for fabricating his
faery language.  He could, then, have made it all up.

Alternatively, of course, we could take him at his word.  The
words he related are of Indo-European origin, but- as I've just
implied- we might very well expect this to be the case.  Gerald
referred to the 'British language' in his passage, by which he
meant the Welsh of his day.  *Ydor* is the faery word for water,
to which we may compare *dower* in Cornish, *dour* in Breton,
*dwfr* or *dŵr* in modern Welsh, and *hudōr* in Greek.  By *halgein*
the faeries meant salt- and in Cornish we find *sal,* in Breton

---

[39] Gerald of Wales, *The Journey through Wales & Description of Wales,*
Penguin, 1987, Book I, chapter 8- or Sikes p.106.

*holen,* in modern Welsh *halen,* in Gaelic *salann* and in Greek *álas.* The congruities are clear; perhaps Elidyr's report tells us something about the very deep roots of Faery speech in Britain. Perhaps it is even as old as Old European.

## Genetics

What of the human population of Britain- how much has that changed over time? The accepted and traditional model of the settlement of the British Isles is of waves of people arriving in boats and conquering and displacing the existing inhabitants. Rarely, perhaps, they interbred, but population replacement was assumed to be the norm. The 'Beaker People' were replaced by the 'Celts,' who in turn were pushed out of the way by a tide of Germanic peoples- Saxons, Angles, Jutes and, later, Vikings.

The genetic evidence does not support this. Across the British Isles as a whole, three quarters of the population descend from people who lived here long before the first farming began in the Neolithic period. Precisely, this applies to 81% of Welsh people, 79% of the Cornish, 70% of Scots and 68% of the English population. This last figure is especially notable- over two thirds of the English, who are supposed to descend from those incoming Anglo-Saxons who massacred and chased off the existing British tribes, in fact have an ancestry dating back thousands of years earlier. Only a tiny percentage of the English gene-pool (5%) derives from later invaders.[40]

Most of the people resident in Britain have been here since Mesolithic times- we are descendants of 'stone age men' rather than marauders in longships. The British relationship with the land- and its other inhabitants- has therefore persisted and developed over millennia. Languages have come and gone, leaving little trace except for a few remnant words

---

[40] S. Oppenheimer, *The Origins of the British- A Genetic Detective Story,* 2006; D. Miles, *The Tribes of Britain,* 2005.

(consider, for example, the speech of the so-called Picts in Scotland: we can infer that it was related to the 'Celtic' languages of Cumbria, Wales and Cornwall, but it has almost entirely vanished in the face of Irish Gaelic and, of course, English).  Nonetheless, the people- and their knowledge, place names and stories- have remained.

The transmission of traditional information continued uninterrupted for many, many centuries.  It is really only over the last two hundred years that this unbroken flow of culture and wisdom has been disrupted.  The Industrial Revolution, and the population movements and urbanisation that resulted from it, severed many people's links to their ancestral birthplaces.  The effects of this deracination were exacerbated by national education and by mass media, which helped to further devalue and obliterate 'old wives' tales' and 'primitive' ideas.

These combined processes risked the total loss of the accumulated knowledge associated with localities. Fortunately, Victorian and early twentieth century folklorists realised what was at risk of being lost and they recorded as much as they could.  Whilst this information is no longer passed on orally, within families and between neighbours and in the physical context in which it was accrued, it has been preserved for us- often through the very media that had initially threatened its survival: books, newspapers, television, radio and the internet.

Summary

In conclusion, our links to the land are deep and ancient. Words and traditions preserve knowledge and experiences from ancestors long past.  Those links may have been weakened during the last two centuries, but we are still able to recover and to understand what they meant to our predecessors.  We can still reconnect to them and to the land that was their home.

One link in that chain must be the faeries, whose heritage seems to be far more stable than our own.  The evidence suggests that we have lived alongside them time out of mind and that our image and understanding of our home has been shaped by their presence- and is inseparable from it.  The following chapters will demonstrate this in more detail.

A wide range of features in the natural world are associated with the Good Neighbours.  They may be found in upland areas, in woodlands, around watery spots (most particularly springs), on islands, and linked to caves and other holes in the ground.  I shall give just a couple of illustrations here.[41]

## Hills

Certain natural mounds or elevations tend to be linked to the Good Folk; most typically these are distinctive round hills, often called 'knowes' in Scots and *sitheans* in Gaelic.  Low, isolated and often verdant, these spots stand out in the landscape as something unusual and special.

Faery hills can be much larger than mere mounds, though, as demonstrated firstly by the village of Strontian in Sunart in the Highlands, the name of which derives from the Gaelic name for a local feature, *Sròn an t-Sìthein*- 'the nose, or point,' of the faery hill.'   Secondly, in Perthshire there is the mountain called Schiehallion, in Gaelic *Sìth Chailleann*, or the 'fairy hill of Caledonia.'

More than just their names, faery legend attaches to both these sites too: on Schiehallion, for instance, an encounter took place on a knoll overlooking a small cave, where a man saw the *sith* folk dancing and singing.  The cave is still identifiable today (and is marked on Ordnance Survey maps)- it is *Uamh Tom a' Mhor-fhir,* which lies behind the Allt Mor burn.  With a curious irony, the Gaelic name means 'the Cave of the Big Men,' although its dimensions contradict that.  It's hard to locate in the daylight, even with a map- but finding it may well be easier if you're following the sound of faery voices, as happened in the story.[42]

---

[41] For more detail, see my *Faery* (2020) c.5 and *Faeries & the Natural World* (2021), c.4.

Another group of natural features that have long had magical or supernatural properties associated with them are wells and springs.  Not only are they notable for the fact that we sense the power and abundance of nature very directly in the appearance of fresh water bubbling up from the ground, but these sources not infrequently have magical and healing properties attributed to them, too (as Ithell Colquhoun was aware in Cornwall).

A few examples with suffice: just below the hill fort of Maiden Castle near to Wooler in Northumberland there is a Fairy (or Wishing) Well; the alternative name indicates its use by locals.  The practice used to be for young people to visit on holidays such as May Day when they would drop a crooked pin into the waters and make a wish.  More importantly, weak children used to be dipped in the spring and a gift of bread and cheese would be left for the faery guardians to secure the cure.

In West Penwith in Cornwall there is a Fairy Well on the cliffs east of Carbis Bay where wishes are granted whilst Venton Bebibell (the well of the little people) is to be found on the moors further west, near to the famous Men an Tol holed stone (a monument which is itself associated with a healing faery presence).  Dolls used to be dipped in the spring's waters on Good Friday by local children.

Place Names

My particular interest in this chapter is not so much the types of features with which the faeries are linked as the names the British have given to places in their landscape.  Many of these

---

[42] See MacDougall & Calder, *Folk Tales,* 263; Westwood & Kingshill, *The Lore of Scotland,* 111.

date back to early medieval times and indicate once more the very longstanding faery associations with the land.

Whilst quite a few of these faery names relate to prominent features like hills, streams and pools, many refer to much smaller, less significant and, even, transitory locations.  A large proportion of these are field names- used in the past but highly vulnerable to changes of land-use today.  The consolidation of fields or their conversion to intensive arable have, over the last century, done away with the need to identify various small leys, meadows and such like.  This has put many local faery names at risk.  Subtle landscape features were also labelled, but these highly local names may be forgotten over the generations as our intimate connection to the landscape weakens: Poflet, in Devon, for example, describes a dip down to a stream which Puck frequented; in late Tudor times there was a Hop Gap at Methley in the West Riding of Yorkshire- a space in a fence where you might meet Hob.  Such localised names are very vulnerable to being lost.

I'll start this survey with names including the element 'fairy.' These are, in fact, quite rare and are mostly of rather recent origin, the majority only apparently dating from Victorian times. As readers may be aware, this ought to be expected, in that 'fairy' is a word derived from French and a relative late-comer to the English language.  Confirmed fae origins may be found for Fairy Yard, a field at Ashton on Mersey in Cheshire, the Fairy Close and Hill at Wragby in West Yorkshire and Fairy Cross, at Trent in Dorset.  As the *English Place Name Survey* remarks of these, they seem to denote places renowned for being haunted by faeries.  Interestingly, names incorporating the element 'pixie' are equally rare.  The rectory at Durweston in Dorset is recorded as being named Pexy's Hole, the hollow haunted or frequented by pixies, in 1584.  There are other examples, but these are first recorded at a later date.  As with the more recent 'fairy' names, they therefore suggest a conscious and even romantic choice of label rather than a traditional significance.

Names that include the Anglo-Saxon *aelf*, 'elf,' are also surprisingly absent.  We find that, in 1285, Eldon Hill in Derbyshire was recorded as Elvedon, the elves' hill.  Alfin Hall at Agbrigg in the West Riding speaks for itself.  The lost *Alvehou* at Tetney in Lincolnshire and *Alveleg* at Crich in Derbyshire were the elves' mound and clearing respectively. The 'alvysch thornys'- the 'elves' thorn trees'- were recorded in 1319 as a field name at Milton Abbas in Dorset.

A lot of the apparent 'fairy' place-names actually come from other words such as 'ferry' or 'fair.'  Too ready an interpretation without tracing back the name to its origins can often produce misleading results.  The writer Jabez Allies, in his *Roman and Saxon Antiquities and Folklore of Worcestershire,* of 1856, was rather guilty of this.  His pride in his home county and its rich traditions encouraged him to find faery names everywhere: he enumerated thirty parishes where there are places named after Puck, for instance, and another twenty-six in which the goblin Hob is commemorated. Sadly, modern scholarship is not so generous in its attributions.[43]

Hob is a good example of the potential pitfalls, as many names are more likely to derive from the personal name Hobbe than from the supernatural being.  Nonetheless, at least eighteen 'Hob' names can be identified that are connected to the goblin.  These are concentrated in the north of England and are often related to natural features, such as hills, fields and- in one case- stones, the Hobb Stones at Tankersley in South Yorkshire.  Other names concentrated in the north of England are Boggart and Boggle, applied to fields and woods in West Yorkshire, Cheshire and Westmoreland.  A particular boggart known in the north was 'Old Skrat,' and he is named in at least nine places.[44]

---

[43] Allies, *Roman and Saxon Antiquities and Folklore of Worcestershire*: for Puck see 303, 340, 424 & 466; for Hob see 273, 313-4, 337-40, 413 & 467.
[44] On boggarts & boggles see my Beyond Faery, 2020, c.9.

We'll encounter the Anglo-Saxon *scucca* again later.  This is a sort of goblin now called the 'shuck' or 'shock' and its presence is marked in at least sixteen names, denoting woods, streams, hills and marshes, from the east of England up to Cheshire.  Outliers include Shobrooke in Devon and Shucklow Warren in Buckinghamshire.

The other goblin name with clear Anglo-Saxon roots is 'Puck,' from the Old English *puca*.  This name is the most common in England, being found in at least fifty-three places, of which a third are in Gloucestershire and over seventy per cent in the South and South West of England more broadly.  About a quarter of these names are associated with pits or holes, alongside a scatter of hills, streams, pools, moors and woods.

Summary

In recent years various folklore researchers have commented upon the value of place-names for understanding where and how our ancestors encountered and understood the Good Folk.  They are a valuable resource that opens up for us past contacts and experiences.  There are clearly places that have had a recognised supernatural presence for as much as a thousand years, if not longer.[45]

Combining folklore accounts with the place-name evidence, we find that faery-derived names are scattered across the country but with some counties covered by a web of associations, meaning that in Cheshire and West Yorkshire, for example, you will seldom find yourself far from a site with traditional faery connections.

---

[45] See, for example, Francis Young, *Suffolk Fairylore,* 2019, 13-14 and Simon Young & Ceri Houlbrook, *Magical Folk,* 2018, 29 (Sussex), 33-35 (Worcs), 56 (Yorks), 66-67 & &1 (Dorset) and 83 (Cumbria).

# Ancient Sites

As we saw in the last chapter, natural features alone can produce a 'faery geography' of Britain.  However, the gazetteer is much fuller and richer, creating a mosaic of faery references across the land.

If, as it is only reasonable to suppose, the faery folk have been settled in Britain for thousands of years, various locations will have become especially associated with them.  This, of course, the situation that prevails.  A variety of prehistoric sites are identified as having particular faery associations; these are found across the British Isles.  As one writer observed of ancient sites in Glamorgan in South Wales, "there are *always* fairy tales and ghost stories connected with them…" whilst it has been said that the Cornish spriggans "are found only about the cairns, coits [quoits] or cromlechs, burrows or detached stones, with which it is unlucky for mortals to meddle."[46]

## Archaeological Features

In fact, the majority of locations with faery connections are actually prehistoric monuments, constructed by humans in the Neolithic or early Iron Age.  These include chambered tombs, hill forts, duns, burial mounds, standing stones, stone circles and other arrangements, cairns and brochs.[47]

On the Isle of Skye (and in the western isles more generally) people rightly understood that the Bronze Age duns were faery *sitheans;* they were said to be "as old as the *sithe*"- in other words, they were believed to be older even than human settlement.  As we shall soon see, proper respect for such

---

[46] J. W. Lukis, *Archaeologia Cambrensis,* 4th series, vol.6, 174; Robert Hunt, *Popular Romances of the West of England,* vol.1, 66.
[47] A dun is a fortified settlement; a cairn is a stone burial mound and a broch is a stone tower used as a fortified dwelling.

places is essential.  A man who took building stones from the *sithean* of Dun Gharsainn successively lost his horse, cattle, crops and boat, ultimately being forced to emigrate.  By contrast, a man who stopped his labourers taking materials for a byre from the *sithean* of Dun Taimh was rewarded by its inhabitants with a gift of fifty of the *cu sith,* faery cattle, and the guarantee that they and their descendants would serve his family well for five hundred years.[48]

As the Dun Gharsainn example demonstrates, it is exceedingly unwise to try to take stones from a faery dun or any other such site.  Similar dismal fates befell those who tried to take stones from a broch at Houstry in Caithness or from a cromlech on Guernsey. Indeed, more than just avoiding harm, paying active respect at these locations is advisable.  On the Hebridean island of Luing, for example, travellers passing the faery dun at Dubh-Leister would pull a thread from their clothes and leave it as an offering.  In Lancashire, a boggart was believed to haunt a tumulus near to Over Darwen and, as late as the 1860s, children passing would take off their shoes and clogs so as not to disturb the dreaded being within the mound with the clatter of their feet on the highway.[49]

Usage

A range of faery activities are ascribed to these ancient sites. In around thirty per cent of cases they are identified as faery dwellings.  Thirteen per cent are places where dancing took place and eleven per cent are the venues for fairy celebrations- feasts and other 'revels' (which could well include dancing and music as well).[50]

---

[48] O. Swire, *Skye- The Island and Its Legends,* 1961, 162, 163 & 174; see too Swire's *Inner Hebrides,* 1964 & *Outer Hebrides,* 1966, passim.
[49] 'Sacred Fire,' *Folklore,* vol.9, 1898, 280; Polson, *Our Highland Folklore Heritage,* 1926, 49, 50 & 133-135; Marie de Garis, *Folklore of Guernsey;* Swire, *Inner Hebrides,* 197; C. Hardwick, *Traditions, Superstitions and Folklore (Chiefly of Lancashire and the North of England),* 1872, 141.
[50] These figures are based on an analysis of the sites identified in Leslie

A few examples, based around these varying usages of sites, will illustrate the sorts of faery sightings that have occurred.

Celebrations

As I just stated, about a quarter of the ancient sites that are linked to the faeries are associated with their merrymaking. The barrow known as *Twmpath Dawnsio* (the mound of the dance) at Caerwys in Flintshire is self-explanatory; the Fairy Mount at Wrexham is another prehistoric burial mound, around the base of which the *tylwyth teg* were said to dance and play.  The Carn Gluze barrow near St Just in Cornwall was associated with faery dancing and lights were often seen there at night.  Dances have also been witnessed on Midsummer's Eve at the Tarberry hill fort, near Harting in Sussex and at Cauldon Low hill in Staffordshire.  The latter is commemorated in Mary Howitt's 1847 poem *The Fairies of Cauldon Low- a Midsummer Legend.*  This verse is also an excellent example of one way in which a local faery legend has become part of wider British culture.[51]

The faeries, being "little folk, like girls to look at" have been seen to emerge from a hole in the ground under one of the megaliths so they can dance at the Rollright stone circle in Oxfordshire. The Good Folk are also reported to dance (in circuits of three) around the Hurl Stone at Lilburn in Northumberland, the Blue Stone outside St Andrews, and around the Pembrokeshire cromlechs at Pentre Ifan and on Frenni Fawr mountain (sites which the *tylwyth teg* are said to protect with special care).  The stone circles called the Haltadans on Shetland are famed for the trow dances performed there at the full moon- it is said that the stones are actually unwary trows who were petrified when they were caught still dancing by the rising sun.[52]

---

Grinsell's *Folklore of Prehistoric Sites,* 1974.
[51] In the same county of Staffordshire, the faeries also dance on Christmas Eve at the barrow called Long Low, near Castern Hill.

Banquets have been witnessed (and not infrequently shared in) inside a number of round barrows (which are often seen open and illuminated at night).  Feasting locations include the burial mounds at Willie's Howe in East Yorkshire and Orrisdale on the Isle of Man, but also hillforts, such as Dun Osdale on Skye, and on the tree-covered ridge of Tom Na h-Iubraich near Inverness.  This is the 'knoll or mound of the yew,' a name which also indicates the faery link with that tree (for which, see later).  Lastly, the Ardilistry Stones, the remains of a cairn on Islay, were once the venue for a banquet held by the *sith* folk.

Faery fiddle playing has been heard emanating from the Broch of Houland on Shetland; music is also associated with the dun of Mingulay on Barra, a cairn at Strath and the *sithean* at Pretty Hill, near Braes, both on Skye, as well as a stone circle known as the Lawers Sithean at Kenmore in Perthshire.  In the latter instance, a man passing by followed the music into the *sithean* and, at the end of his visit, was given a white horse that could gallop at astonishing speed by the faeries.

Numerous *tumuli* in Dorset are celebrated as 'music barrows' where, if you sit on their summit at midday, you will hear the sounds rising of faeries playing instruments inside.  These sites include the burial mound on Bottlebrush Down, near Wimbourne, where a curate one evening witnessed "a crowd of little people in leather jerkins" dancing around him.  Others are found at Ashmore, Culliford Tree, Bincombe Bumps, Whitcombe and the Fairy Toot at Butcombe (where children also used to see visions in the bushes growing on the chambered tomb).  Music is heard as well under the ground after darkness at Wick Barrow near Stogursey in Somerset.  This *tumulus* is also known locally as the Pixies' Mound; like Beedon Barrow (discussed later), if any earth or stone from it is moved during the day it will return to its original location

---

[52] L. Spence, *British Fairy Origins*, 1946, 182-3; Sikes, *British Goblins,* 380; Westwood & Kingshill, *The Lore of Scotland,* 389-91.

overnight.  Furthermore, the mound is the setting for a story about a ploughman who mended the pixies' broken 'peel' (a large wooden tool used for lifting items in and out of an oven) and was rewarded with a freshly baked cake.[53]

On Skye there is a *sithean* known as Aant Sidhe near Strath. As a double confirmation of its nature, perhaps, this is a mound which is topped with a standing stone.  The resident faeries were reported to emerge and dance around it on moonlit nights and, at other times, their music could be heard inside.[54]

At Pudding Pie Hill, a round barrow at Sowerby in East Yorkshire, it was the faeries themselves who could be heard. Daring individuals who ran around the hillock nine times and then stuck a knife in the top and placed their ear to the ground, would be able to listen in on the conversation of the faeries residents inside.

Domestic Dwellings

As stated, most ancient sites are merely identified as faery dwellings.  The hill fort of Caer Drewyn near Corwen in Wales is said to be the home of the faery king, Gwynn ap Nudd. Forts and numerous barrows are the conventional locations for residences (their resemblance to natural hillocks must be a very important factor in this), but less conventional spots include the stone circle at Elva Hill (Elfhow) in Northumberland.

Beedon Barrow in Berkshire is a fairy inhabited tumulus that's notable for two reasons: firstly, it is immune to human interference.  It can never be reduced by ploughing, no materials can ever be removed from it, nor can it be opened- a thunderstorm will immediately follow.  Secondly, a farmer who broke his plough near the barrow found that it had been

---

[53] Westwood & Simpson, *The Lore of the Land,* 209 & 15.
[54] Swire, *Skye- The Island and Its Legends,* 219.

repaired for him by the faeries whilst he was absent fetching his own tools.  Usually, ploughmen feature in stories in which they mend broken items for the faery folk; in this case, the inhabitants of the barrow seem to be self-sufficient and skilled.  Sometimes, though, the help offered by the inhabitants of ancient sites can be too generous and too enthusiastic.  There are Scottish stories, associated with the duns at Bhuirg on Mull and at Borve, at Snizort near Portree on Skye, where the fae folk quickly completed all the weaving that needed to be done and then demanded more work.  The human host was only able to get rid of them by crying out that their home was on fire.[55]

It is commonly understood in British faerylore that the faeries prefer to live underground.  Hence a *fogou* (a prehistoric subterranean passage) near Constantine in mid-Cornwall was named 'the pixie house.'  The antiquarian John Aubrey recorded how a shepherd was taken from one of the burial mounds on Hackpen Hill in Wiltshire to "strange places underground," where he saw the faeries playing music on instruments that resembled viols and lutes.[56]

Ancient standing stones often mark the access to Faery- as appears to be the case at the Rollright stones, noted earlier. A common account found throughout the British Isles describes a hole or stairs beneath a *menhir* that will lead to the faery realm- an excellent example being the Welsh story of Einion and Olwen, in which the mortal boy first enters faeryland by means of some steps that he discovers located beneath a tall stone standing in a rushy place surrounded by faery rings.[57]  Although they sound rather less accommodating, *menhirs* such as that entered by Einion can also constitute the actual faery dwellings, as is the case with

---

[55] See, for example, MacCulloch, *The Misty Isle of Skye,* 1929, 241 & Swire, *Skye- The Island and Its Legends,* 79.
[56] Aubrey, *Remains of Gentilisme,* 1688, 30; Westwood, *Lore of the Land,* 786.
[57] Evans Wentz, *Fairy Faith in Celtic Countries,* 161.

the Hoston or Humberstone in Leicestershire and St John's Stone in the city of Leicester itself (which local children used once to avoid at night because that was when the faeries came out to dance).  Understandably- and just like the Welsh cromlechs noticed earlier- the faes will protect these stones, so that a farmer who carelessly broke off part of the Humberstone when ploughing was reduced from prosperity to poverty and died in the workhouse.[58]

The mention earlier of the 'pixie house' reminds us that these sites will bear a variety of labels that demonstrate their associations with the supernatural population more generally. In Deepdale in Derbyshire there is a *tumulus* called Hob Hurst's House.  The cairn known as Obtrush Rook in Yorkshire is another hobgoblin's home.  Likewise, Shucklow Warren, the goblin's barrow, is derived from the Anglo-Saxon *scuccan hlaew* (commemorating the faery beast still known in East Anglia as the shuck or shock).[59]

Two curiously named sites may have gained their names because they were suggestive of domestic comfort and rest. At Hetton-le-Hole in County Durham there is an ancient barrow called the Fairies' Cradle.  It is a site where the Good Folk were known to assemble for moonlight dances.  Near Hutton Mills in Berwickshire are located two cairns called Cradle Knowes, in which the faeries live.

Food

As well as being associated with the consumption of food at banquets and feasts, a number of prehistoric sites have links to other aspects of the faeries and their food supply, such as its sale and storage.

---

[58] Westwood, *Lore of the Land,* 422-3 & 425; L. Spence, *The Minor Traditions of British Mythology,* 1948, 143.
[59] See my *Beyond Faery,* 2020.

The barrows at Otterford in Somerset, which are known as Robin Hood's Butts, are the site of a famous faery market. South Cadbury hill fort, which also has very strong Arthurian links (as we shall see later), was used to store corn by the local faeries.  The installation of bells in a nearby church drove them away, although they allegedly left their gold behind them (see the following section).

A curious story comes from Stapeley Hill near Corndon in Shropshire.  Here there's a stone circle known as Mitchell's Fold.  A magical cow appeared at this spot in a time of dire drought and famine. She had been sent by the faery queen to feed the local people until conditions improved; a faery woman had been turned into a cow for the duration, apparently (not a pleasant experience, presumably, but such is the power of the faery queen over her subjects). The cow would appear twice a day to supply all the local households with their needs- so long as they weren't greedy or selfish and only came to fill one receptacle for each household each day. Eventually, a witch (called Mitchell in some versions) arrived for her share of the bounty; however, she had replaced the bottom of her pail with a sieve. The faery cow soon realised it was being abused; firstly, she kicked the witch, so that she became rooted to the ground. Then the cow disappeared, leaving the local people bereft- for you should never exploit or take advantage of faery generosity. In revenge, a cairn or ring of stones was erected around the witch who had injured her neighbours so cruelly. Strictly, of course, this site commemorates a site of faery bounty rather than their residence, but they were clearly present and very active in the vicinity.[60]

Other Uses

Lastly, a number of sites have more unusual faery links.  As at South Cadbury, faery gold is also buried in the hill fort of Bury Ditches in Shropshire.  An interest in precious metals might

---

[60] *Byegones,* July 1893, 118-119; Henry Bett, *English Myths & Traditions,* 1952, 45.

explain why the Manx faeries used a tunnel that connected Shan Cashtal hill fort with the churchyard at Maughold, near to which is an old mine shaft (but then again, flint mining is said to have driven the faeries out of the Iron Age enclosure they had occupied at Harrow Hill in Sussex).

If you run nine times without stopping around the barrow at Newport Pagnell in Buckinghamshire, the faeries will appear to you.  This could prove to be an alarming experience, but on Shetland the cairns known as the Rounds of Tivla have an opposite effect: walk alone around them at midnight and you will never again feel fear in the presence of the trows.

Lastly, John Aubrey tells of the large stone lying in a "cavous place" at Borough-hill near Frensham, Surrey.  Music was heard here, but the site's primary significance was that locals could knock upon the stone and declare whatever they wished to borrow- whether oxen, money, a cauldron or any other useful object.  A fairy voice would then tell them when to come back to the spot, on which occasion the item would be there, being loaned for up to a year or more, conditional upon its return.[61]

We have so far discussed the faeries' use of ancient sites but, given the supernatural link to standing stones and *tumuli*, it was inevitable that people would invest these sites with magical powers, just as they do with natural sites like wells.  We have seen the curative properties of *Men an Tol;* conversely in Ireland and Scotland interference with or damage to stones was avoided through fear of fairy revenge.  In Ireland the belief persists that disturbance could lead either to crops or the home burning.  In the Scottish Highlands the Reverend Robert Kirk recorded a prohibition upon taking turf or wood from a *sithbruaich* (a fairy hill); similarly, tethering an animal by pinning it down on the knoll was very unpopular with the fairy inhabitants within.[62]

---

[61] Aubrey, *Natural History of Surrey,* vol.3, 366.
[62] Campbell, *Superstitions of the Highlands and Islands of Scotland,* c.1.

Origins

As we now appreciate, almost all of these faery-inhabited sites were once constructed or occupied by humans.  The tiny handful of exceptions are White Catherton hillfort in Tayside, which was built by a witch as a faery stronghold, the hill fort of Cow Castle on Exmoor which built by the faeries themselves as a defence against 'earth spirits' reportedly, and Pudding Pie Hill barrow, which was mentioned earlier.[63]

In the other cases, what was once a place used by mortals has now been appropriated by the Good Neighbours.  There seem to be several explanations for why this might be so.  Frequently, the locations are convenient just sites that can be taken over at minimal effort by the faeries.  In fact, their occupation has now lasted so long that the human origin of the sites is lost to folk memory.  Instead, they have become mysterious and (quite often) scary.  By way of example, *Caer yr Ellyllon* (the Elves' Cairn) near Mold in Clwyd and the cairn known as the Fairy Knowe at Stenton in Lothian were both sites that were avoided at night by children because they were afraid of being taken by the fae.  We might even propose that these monuments, being so old and ruinous, had taken on something of the quality of natural features and so were regarded by people as faery dwellings for that reason alone.

Meet the Ancestors

In truth, it is not only the faeries who inhabit these sites.  It is common in folk tradition to come across cases where individuals who have visited or stumbled into Faery are

---

[63] In Westwood & Simpson, *The Lore of the Land,* 2005, 641, it is speculated that these earth spirits are akin to the spriggans of Cornwall, who lived in hillfort, such as Trencrom Hill, near St Ives, where they hoarded their gold.

surprised to discover that there are humans living there as well- people that they had thought to be dead.

Several instances may be noted.  The Scottish tale of the *Tacksman of Auchriachan* relates how a tenant farmer in search of some lost goats came upon a strange house where he was surprised to meet a woman whose funeral he had only recently attended.  As is often the case, she had been abducted by the *sith* people under the guise of her death to serve as their housekeeper.  An almost identical discovery is man by a lost man in the Cornish story of the *Faery Dwelling on Silena Moor.*  In another story from the Highlands, a man saw a group of faeries spinning wool, amongst whom was a local woman who had died a hundred years previously.  An account very typical of a collection of reports concerns Katharine Fordyce, from the Isle of Unst in the Shetlands, who was taken by the trows immediately after her child was born and was later seen by a neighbour, trapped inside a faery hill.  Many women have been abducted in comparable circumstances, although- unlike Katharine- some have been able to return home and others have been rescued.[64]

These are folk accounts, but we also have the recorded testimony of women accused of witchcraft who had comparable experiences.  For instance, Bessie Dunlop was contacted by the faeries through an emissary they sent to her, a man called Thom Reid who had died in battle thirty years previously.  Bessie later saw a faery rade gallop past and one of the party was a local laird, deceased four years earlier.  Another suspected witch, Elspeth Reoch, in 1616 claimed to have met "ane farie man" who turned out to be a murdered relative of hers, called John Stewart.  A third accused witch, Alesoun Pearson, also met two dead noblemen when she visited Faery.[65]

---

[64] J. F. Campbell, *Popular tales of the West Highlands,* vol.2, 65; Edmondson & Saxby, *Home of a Naturalist,* 1888, 207.
[65] Pitcairn, *Ancient Criminal Trials,* vol.1, part 2, 49-58; Black, *Examples of Printed Folklore Concerning Orkney and the Shetland Islands,* 1903, 111;

A true sense of the antiquity of the faeries comes from Cornwall, where the little folk, the *pobel vean,* are sometimes also referred to as the 'Old People.'  The name reflects a local belief that the peninsula's faeries were, in fact, the spirits of virtuous druids from the distant past.  The same explanation for the presence of the *tylwyth teg* was found in Wales.  These ideas are of particular significance to the faeries' connection with ancient sites, for before the nineteenth century all ancient monuments tended to be ascribed to 'the druids.'[66]

The presence of 'ancestors,' of members of previous generations, who are found to be living alongside the faery folk, will no doubt have reinforced people's sense that their Good Neighbours were a longstanding presence in the British Isles.  Perhaps even more importantly (*a fortiori* where there was passage back and forth between the realms), knowledge of this human presence in Faery may have enhanced the understanding that this was a shared- and even collaborative- occupation of the land, sustained over thousands of years by mortals and supernaturals together.

Conclusions

Whatever the precise reasons for ancient monuments originally being treated as faery sites, the key aspect of the belief is that it creates a deep link between the landscape and the faery folk.  In addition, it integrates with our history as well as with landforms, explaining the presence of mysterious mounds or standing stones and giving continuity.  Not only might the faeries be in-dwelling in wells, springs and hills, they

---

Sir Walter Scott, *Border Minstrelsy,* vol.2, 340 & Robert Sempill, *The Legend of the Bishop of St. Androis Lyfe, Callit Mr. Patrick Adamsone*; see also the poem *Sir Orfeo,* in which many people who have died young are found in Faery.
[66] Briggs, *Dictionary of Fairies,* 317; Robert Hunt, *Popular Romances of the West of England,* 'The Elfin Creed;' Evans Wentz, *The Fairy Faith in Celtic Countries,* 147,

inhabited the oldest built structures in the country as well, emphasising the extent to which they are embedded within our topography, mythology and culture.

What is perhaps surprising in all of this is the fact that faery legends are *not* attached to any of the most famous prehistoric sites in Britain: there is plenty of mythology surrounding places such as Avebury, Stonehenge, the Uffington White Horse and the chalk cut giants at Cerne Abbas and Wilmington, but none of it is faery related.  Perhaps the very fame of these sites, and the fact that they have long been tourist destinations, explains this otherwise curious neglect.  The Good Folk are, as a rule, a retiring and private people, and the persistent disturbance associated with these sites may have caused them to move away.

Not only are the faeries present in the structures and geomorphology of the British Isles, they have a significant presence in its flora too.  I have described their relationship to plant life, especially to trees such as the elder and rowan, several times elsewhere and here focus on three new examples.[67]

## Yew Trees

In the previous chapter, I noted the faery link with yew trees indicated by the dun at *Tom na h-Iubraich* (Tomnahurich) in Inverness-shire.  This hill, crowned by a yew, is the setting for a famous story of two Strathspey fiddlers who were offered a double fee to pay at a celebration being held within the mound.  It was an offer they could hardly refusal and they played all night.  Emerging the next morning, they made their way back to their homes in Inverness, where they were shocked to discover that everything had changed.  They had been absent for a hundred years, rather than a night, and quickly crumbled away to dust.[68]

In Britain, yew trees are closely associated with churchyards. It's sometimes said that this was ordained because yew wood was ideal for longbows, so that English kings wanted to preserve the trees by planting them in a protected environment. This is a nice story, but it's plainly wrong, as very many yews far older than the Middle Ages can be found growing around churches, in addition to which they are to be found growing by wells and on ancient sites such as hill forts. Their significance stretches back much further than the Hundred Years War and is by no means linked to the Christian church.

---

[67] See my *Faery,* 2020 and *Faeries & the Natural World,* 2021.
[68] Westwood & Kingshill, *Lore of Scotland,* 451; T. Keightley, *Fairy Mythology,* 1850, 387.

An example of such a tree grows within the boundary of the church of Hope Bagot near Ludlow in Shropshire. The Hope Bagot yew is monumental: it's about eight metres or twenty-five feet in circumference, very obviously of great age- at least one thousand years- and its canopy extends over a huge area, shading far more than the small bubbling well beneath its roots. It's a remarkable sight and easily attests to the awe-inducing majesty of these long-lived trees.

Yews are not regularly associated with faeries, unlike rowans and elders, but there are several British accounts that demonstrate that these significant trees very properly do have supernatural associations. This is because they have magical properties that make them significant to the faes.[69]

Firstly, I have recounted elsewhere the story of the malicious water sprite that lived in a pool at Marden in Herefordshire.[70] Through some accident now forgotten, the church bell had rolled into the pool and had been captured by the maid. Horses tried to drag it out, but failed, and the villagers were advised by a 'wise man' that the job could only be accomplished using a team of sterile cows (called freemartins), which was to be equipped with yokes made from two magical woods- from yew fitted with bands of rowan (some accounts also say that the drivers had whips whose handles were made from rowan). The recovery itself had to be performed in silence. Everything was going well, with the bell being hauled steadily out of the mud, the water sprite being fast asleep inside, when one of the men cried out in excitement. The faery promptly awoke and plunged back into the pool, dragging the bell with her. She angrily cried out that she'd have drowned the team as well, had not the magical woods prevented her:

---

[69] Yews appear in Irish legend too, linked with the Tuatha De Danann- for example, Fer Hi (yew man) son of Fogabal (yew tree fork) who was the king of the *sidhe* of Cnoc Aine.
[70] See, for example, my *Beyond Faery,* 2020.

"If it had not been
For your wittern [rowan] bands
And your yew tree pin
I should have had your twelve freemartins in."

The second instance of a faery association with yew comes from Mathafarn, in Powys in mid-Wales. A story describes an abduction in a faery ring that occurred there in the Ffridd yr Ywen (the Yew Forest). Two farm labourers, Twm and Iago (Tom and Jack), were working in the wood one summer's day when a mist descended. They thought evening had come and had set off homewards, when they came across the yew that gave the wood its name, right at the heart of the forest. This was at a spot called the 'Dancing Place of the Goblin,' and the clearing was filled with a strange light. The glow persuaded the pair that it was not as late as they'd thought and they decided to take a nap there. When Twm woke up, Iago had disappeared- abducted in a dance of the *tylwyth teg* under the yew tree. The rest of the story concerns Iago's rescue, although this proves ultimately tragic: once he is pulled back into the world of men a whole year later, he eats food and crumbles away (rather like the Inverness fiddlers).[71]

The last yew-tree story takes us to Scotland. It describes the *glaistig* of Morvern. who haunted a lonely area of mountain, known as the *Garbh-shlios*, a rough stretch of country that extends along the west coast from the Sound of Mull to Kingairloch- a total distance of about seven miles. Here the *glaistig* herded sheep and cattle over the wild pastures. She was said to be a small, but very strong, woman and she would take refuge at night in a particular yew tree (*craobh iuthair*), for protection from the wild animals that prowled around beneath. The *glaistig* once competed with a local man rowing a coracle across to the island of Lismore. He had thought himself to be a good rower, and he felt ashamed when he was bested by a woman- but he confessed that he never rowed so hard in all

---

[71] Wirt Sikes, *British Goblins,* 73.

his life. When the boat reached the other shore, the mysterious little woman vanished and he realised he had tested his strength against the *glaistig*.[72]

What can be said in conclusion about yews in British faerylore? It's evidently a wood with magical properties, one that can repel faes in the same way as rowan but which can also provide them with shelter. This is a contradictory nature-puzzling, but typically faery too. The trees' magical power also protects and even sanctifies wells and other ancient sites.

Oak Trees

The oak tree has held a magical and spiritual status in European culture for a very long time indeed.  The Greek nymphs known as dryads derived their name from the oak trees in which they lived (although, interestingly, Robert Graves decided to gloss their name as 'oak tree fairy' in English).  The dryads are the spirits of the trees themselves, living within them, and it is not always clear from British sources whether or not our own oak trees are animate or have an indwelling sprite.  Furthermore, a root word related to dryad provided us with druid, the ancient British priests of the oak groves, highlighting their ancient sanctity in these isles.[73]

We must note the experience of Bishop Richard Corbet (author of the poem *Rewards and Fairies*), who became lost near Bosworth in 1640.  To find their way again, he and his party were advised to:

> "Turne your cloakes,
> … for Pucke is busy in these oakes.

---

[72] J. G. Campbell, *Superstitions of the Highlands & Islands of Scotland*, 1900, 173.

[73] R. Graves, *The White Goddess,* 1961, 441; K. Briggs, *The Fairies in Tradition & Literature,* 1967, 83; L. Spence, *The Minor Traditions of British Mythology,* 1948, 109-110; J. Bowker, *Goblin Tales of Lancashire,* 'The Demon of the Oak.'

> If ever wee at Bosworth will be found
> Then turn your cloakes, for this is fairy ground."[74]

The rhyming proverb, 'Fairy folks are in old oaks' survives still and the idea of an oak tree faery remained potent enough for Beatrix Potter to make use of the 'oak-men' in her children's book *The Fairy Caravan* in 1952.

Twenty years later, folklorist Ruth Tongue, in her *Forgotten Folk-Tales of the English Counties* (1970), told the story of 'The Vixen and the Oak-men,' which- like the *Fairy Caravan*- is set in the Lake District.  A vixen travels through dangerous woods, avoiding the evil holly tree, so that she can warn the oak-men that humans are coming to cut the mistletoe from their Great Oak. These oak-men are portrayed as kindly dwarves who serve as forest guardians.  Tongue seems to have derived her oak-men from Beatrix Potter, who may in turn have received her inspiration not from folklore but from several children's books by William Canton- fairy stories he wrote for his daughter.  Canton's oak-men dress in green and live behind little doors at the bottom of trees (possibly the first appearance of 'fairy doors').  Although all the details of these characters are likely to be the invention of Potter, Tongue and, particularly, Canton, they were not invented purely for children; the name itself and the tradition it preserves *are* ancient and authentic.[75]

In *The Discovery of Witchcraft* of 1584 Reginald Scot listed the many different types of faeries with which mothers would scare their children.  He included 'the man in the oke,' a supernatural whose characteristics and habits are now almost entirely lost to us, although a modern witness in Somerset has described the 'oak men' as being small (between two to three feet in height), hairy, and with round eyes, pointed ears, long

---

[74] Corbet, *Iter Boreale,* in *Certain elegant poems, written by Dr. Corbet, Bishop of Norwich*, 1647.
[75] W. Canton, *W. V.: Her Book* (1896), *A Child's Book of Saints* (1898) & *In Memory of W. V.* (1901).

noses and tails.  They live in the hollows in the trunks of old trees and are "generally friendly."  Almost certainly borrowing from Scot, Michael Aislabie Denham included the "men-in-the-oak" in his exhaustive list of faery types in the mid-nineteenth century- but had nothing to add to the name.[76]

That oak trees have a special status as places for faery dancing, or as their dwellings, is well known in British tradition.  Faeries have certainly been seen dancing under oaks in Lancashire, East Yorkshire and in Mid and South Wales.  One Borders story of a *howdie* (midwife) called to assist a birth in a cottage that's strange to her involves the typical incident of faery ointment being applied accidentally to human eyes.  When this happens, the house vanishes and the woman perceives that she is actually in the open, sheltered only by the boughs of an ancient oak tree, its moss-covered trunk being what she had previously mistaken for a fireplace.[77]

In the grounds of Downing House near Whiteford, North Wales, there is a large 'faery oak.'  When a child suddenly becomes peevish and is suspected of being a changeling, if it is left out overnight beneath the tree's boughs, the faeries will have returned the human infant by the next morning.[78]  A particularly informative source on the relationship between the Welsh faeries (the *tylwyth teg*) and oaks is the Welsh minister, the Reverend Edmund Jones. In his 1780 history of the superstitions of Aberystruth parish in Monmouthshire, he recorded the contemporary local views on the most likely locations for seeing faeries.  They do not like stony, plain or marshy places, he reported, but for their dancing preferred those sites that are open, dry and clean and that are near to, or shaded by, the spreading branches of trees, particularly

---

[76] Scot, *Discoverie,* Book VII, c.15; J. Dathen *Somerset Fairies and Pixies,* 2010, 21; *Denham Tracts,* Folklore Society, 1892 & 1895.
[77] Nicholson *Folklore of East Yorkshire* 82; Spence, *British Fairy Origins,* 186; E. Jones, *Appearance of Evil*, no.57 & 116; H. Bett, *English Myths & Traditions,* 1952, 23.
[78] Thomas Pennant, *The History of the Parishes of Whiteford & Holywell,* 1796, 5-6.

those of hazel and female oaks.  Cutting down oak trees can lead to faery retribution, either death or "a strange aching pain which admitted no remedy."[79]

Lastly, a form of sympathetic magic used to be practiced on the east coast of Scotland.  Accepting that the faeries had a strong connection with the trees, the custom once was for families to cut oak and ivy branches in March.  These were then woven into garlands and preserved in the home until the autumn.  If anyone in the family started to look lean, or like they were pining away (as a result, it was assumed, of malign faery influence), they would be passed three times through the garland for a cure.[80]

Hawthorns

The hawthorn (which is also called the whitethorn or may) is a shrubby tree that grows readily and is, consequently, very common throughout Britain.  What's more, it has extremely close links with the faery folk, which can be traced in ballad and stories, as well as in local traditions.

Hawthorns have some general associations with the faes.  For example, one elderly Northumberland man, speaking in the very early eighteenth century, reported that "there was a time when there was not a solitary hawthorn tree out on the green hills, standing amid its circuit of fine cropped grass, that was not witness to the fairy revel and dance held beneath its encircling branches in the twilight or by the pale light of the moon."[81]  In the Scots ballad *Sir Cawline,* the knight has to prove his love to the king's daughter by waiting at night beneath a thorn tree on the Eldridge Hill.  An eldritch knight (who we may understand to be the king of elf-land) then

---

[79] E. Jones, *Relation*, 47-48, *Aberystruth,* 76 & *Appearance of Evil*, no.57 & 116.
[80] Crofton Croker, *Fairy Legends,* 41.
[81] *Denham Tracts,* vol.2, 136, citing Rev. John Horsley, *Materials for a History of Northumberland* (1729-30).

appears and fights Sir Cawline. Thirdly, in the traditions of the Scottish western isles, the cuckoo, a faery bird, naturally lives in hawthorn bushes because they're faery trees. We might note also that, in England, the Derbyshire place name Shuckstonefield was recorded as Schochetorp in the Domesday Book in 1086; this Anglo-Saxon name has the meaning 'the goblin's thorn bush' (and a similar name was noted under 'Domestic Dwellings' in the previous chapter).[82]

Faery encounters are reported to have taken place in the vicinity of thorns too. The Scottish witch suspect, Bessie Dunlop of Lyne in Ayrshire (whom we met earlier), reported two such incidents during her trial in 1576. She was visited repeatedly by a man, Thom Reid, who had died and gone to Faery; one of these meetings took place near the 'Thorne of Damwstarnok.' Secondly, the lord of Auchenskeigh- who had been dead for four years- was seen by Bessie riding with the faery rade past a thorn tree. It seems highly significant as well that this laird's title derives from a Gaelic word meaning 'thorn tree farm.'[83]

In another Scottish ballad, that of *Thomas of Erceldoune,* the hero finds himself "in a mery morning of May/ By Huntlee bankes myself allone." He lies down to rest "undyrnethe a seemly tree" and then sees the faery queen come riding past. It's been suggested, very reasonably, that the tree beneath which Thomas witnesses his vision is "almost certainly a hawthorn."[84] Such an assumption is strengthened if we consider the story associated with Hawthorn Hill in Berkshire. A poor man who lived by the hill had a dream telling him that, if he travelled to London and waited on London Bridge, he would learn something that would make him rich. Seemingly

---

[82] Child Ballad no.6; Spence, *British Fairy Origins,* 186 & *The Fairy Tradition in Britain,* 1948, 321; Henderson & Cowan, *Scottish Fairy Belief,* 2001, 40; O. Swire, *Outer Hebrides & Legends,* 1966, 28; D. Hooke, 'Trees in Anglo-Saxon England,' *Anglo-Saxon Studies* 13, 238.
[83] Pitcairn's *Ancient Criminal Trials,* vol.1, Part 2, 52 & 58; Henderson & Cowan, *Scottish Fairy Belief,* 41.
[84] Henderson & Cowan, *Scottish Fairy Belief,* 2001, 69.

having nothing to lose, the man made the journey and loitered fruitlessly on the bridge for some time.  Eventually, he was approached by a local to ask why he was simply standing there.  The Berkshire man recounted his dream, in response to which the Londoner laughed and said that *he'd* had a dream telling him to go and dig under a hawthorn tree somewhere in Berkshire, but he was too sensible and busy a person to waste his time like that.  The visitor thanked him for the advice and hurried home.  Digging on the hill, he found a pot full of gold- what's more, it bore a Latin inscription which, when translated, informed him that there was 'another, twice as good,' in the same spot.[85]  Almost identical stories are told in respect of a Devonshire man who finds a crock of gold under a thorn bush at Doble's Cross and of a poor pedlar from Swaffham in Norfolk, who is told to dig under an oak tree in an orchard in the village.[86]

Several details seem to interlink all these accounts.  The faeries are often known to communicate with individuals through their dreams, especially those who are asleep under particular trees, and they will frequently use these dreams to direct those dreamers to buried gold.  In the ballad *Sir Orfeo*, the knight's wife is abducted to Faery after sleeping beneath an *ymp tree*, a grafted apple, and it could well be the case that Thomas of Erceldoune made himself vulnerable in the same way by dozing off beneath that hawthorn on the Eildon Hills.  It seems highly relevant, therefore, that in the Berkshire, Devon and Norfolk stories, the gold was buried beneath two thorns and an oak.[87]

Finally, we might note how the artist Ithell Colquhoun reported often seeing a blue mist rising above a thorn tree in a meadow near her home at Lamorna.  It was an "impalpable blue, like wood smoke" visible in all seasons and weathers.  She

---

[85] H. Bett, *English Legends,* 1950, 36; Westwood & Simpson, *Lore of the Land,* 21.
[86] Westwood & Simpson, *Lore of the Land,* 191 & 517.
[87] See too my *Faery Mysteries,* 2022, Part Two.

speculated that it was nature spirits or, perhaps, the remnant of a druid spell.[88]



Hawthorns are prolific and widespread, but they are not especially long-lasting trees.  The other two trees discussed here, though, can be remarkably long lived.  For example, the Bowthorpe Oak, growing at Bourne, Lincolnshire, is estimated to be one thousand years old, and the Minchenden (or Chandos) Oak, in Southgate, London, is believed to be around 800 years old. The famous Major Oak of Sherwood Forest, Nottinghamshire, where Robin Hood is said once to have sheltered, is of similar age to these two.  As for yews, they may have even greater longevity.  They easily survive for between four and six hundred years but a few can last much longer.  Ten yew trees in Britain are believed to date from before the tenth century CE, amongst them the Fortingall Yew in Perthshire, Scotland, which may be two to three thousand years old and the Llangernyw yew in Clwyd, Wales, reckoned to be about one thousand five hundred years old.

The significance of these dates is that- like the prehistoric sites with which faeries may be associated- they indicate a remarkable permanence and fixity within the landscape. Further confirmation of this comes from remarks often made by faery changelings when they are tricked by humans into exposing themselves as interlopers.  One of the most common methods for doing this is the so-called 'brewery of eggshells,' which involves a parent making a show of cooking food in empty egg-shells rather than in pots and pans.  The aim is to pique the fairy's interest and to get him to reveal himself (and his age).  This is frequently expressed by the faery in figurative terms: "I have seen the first acorn before the oak, but I have never seen brewing done in eggshells before!"  A Welsh instance provoked an exclamation in rhymed and

---

[88] Colquhoun, *Living Stones,* 54.

metrical verse (in both the original Welsh *and* in our English translation) from the elderly faery cuckoo:

> "Acorns before oak I knew;
> An egg before a hen;
> Never one hen's egg-shell stew-
> Enough for harvest men!"[89]

Given what's just been said about oaks' longevity, a very long life-span is plainly being implied if the fae had been around to see the acorn germinate.

From time to time, though, the changeling is more precise than these general statements.  A blacksmith of Crosbrig on the Isle of Islay lost his son to the faeries and was advised to confirm the abduction with the eggshell trick.  The changeling declared that "I am now eight hundred years of age, and I have never seen the like of that before."  In one case on Guernsey, a woman cooking limpets in their shells provoked the changeling into exclaiming that:

> "I'm not of this year, nor the year before,
> Nor yet of the time of King John of yore,
> But in all my days and years, I ween,
> So many pots boiling I've never seen."

This may indicate and age of five or six hundred years, but in another example, the changeling claimed to be fifteen hundred years old.  These long lifespans, during which forests have risen and fallen, underline the faeries- deep ties to- and intimate knowledge of- the land that they inhabit.[90]

---

[89] Briggs, *Dictionary of Fairies,* 71; 'Egg Shell Pottage,' *The Cambrian Quarterly Magazine & Celtic Repertory,* vol.2, 1829-30, 86-87; see too Brett, *English Myths,* 31-2, O. Swire, *Inner Hebrides and their Legends,* 1964, 148, and J. Rhys, *Celtic Folklore,* 62, 221, 223, 265 & 268-9.
[90] J. F. Campbell, *Popular Tales of the West Highlands,* vol.2, no.28, p.48; E. MacCulloch, *Guernsey Folklore,* 1908, 219; Harte, *Explore Fairy Traditions,* 115 & 117.

The stories of King Arthur, also known as the 'Matter of Britain,' function at numerous levels, as epic romance, as religious or moral primer, as fairy tale, as history and as a mystical geography of the British Isles.  In the last case, the stories seem to have a serious flaw, in that they comprise a kind of magical gazetteer, yet it is one that contains almost no place-names.  We know of Tintagel, Arthur's birthplace; otherwise, Camelot, site of his court, Camlann, place of his final, fatal battle, and Avalon, his last resting place, are named but not located, and controversy still rages over their identity.  Beyond that, one of Britain's greatest heroes can seem strangely rootless in his own land.[91]

In fact, that inability to finally pin Arthur down to a specific location can be part of the abiding power of his legend.  As will become clear, my interest here is in Arthur's last resting place.  According to the several versions of the story, after Arthur was mortally wounded fighting his traitorous nephew Mordred, he was carried away to Avalon to be healed by the fay maidens Morgan and Nimue.  This account established, early on, a link between the king and the faeries, something which has matured into the human king's faery nature.

Because it was uncertain whether or not Arthur had actually died, the story of his life ended inconclusively- or is still ongoing.  If there was no grave, it followed that there would be a place where he was still alive.  If he was living, the great warrior might return, and be the saviour- once again- of his people.  This hope was preserved initially in the native British areas of Britain- that is, Cornwall, Wales and Cumbria- but it soon became a myth for all inhabitants of the entire land.  When, in 1150, the historian Wace wrote his *Roman de Brut,* he recorded that Arthur "is yet in Avalon, awaited by the

---

[91] See my *Who's Who in Faeryland,* Green Magic Publishing, 2022, c.7 'King Arthur.'

Britons; for, as they say and deem, he will return from whence he went and live again." A few years later, in his own history of England called the *Brut,* the monk Layamon clarified the king's status:

> *"Bruttes ileveð ȝete þat he beon on live,*
> *And wunnien in Avalun mid fairest alre alfen..."*

> "The British believe yet that he is alive,
> And dwells in Avalon with the fairest of all the elves."

By 1190, therefore, it was well established that Arthur had not been killed and was with the faeries. Views have changed little subsequently. In 1578 the historian Raphael Holinshed reported the popular belief that "King Arthur was not dead, but carried away by the fairies into some pleasant place..." In fact, the poet John Lydgate had already elaborated upon this idea- and its implications- over a hundred and fifty years previously:

> "He is a king y-crowned in Faërie,
> With his sceptre and pall, and, with his regalty,
> Shalle resort, as lord and sovereigne,
> Out of Faërie and reign in Bretaine,
> And repair again the oulde Rounde table."[92]

Arthur now partook of the faeries' own nearly immortal nature and was merely biding his time, awaiting his nation's hour of greatest need.

As part of the same process, the faery nature of Arthur's entire court and reign became more apparent with hindsight. Lancelot had been raised by a fae lake woman; Sir Gawain was tested by the green faery knight and Merlin was tempted by Nimue/ Vivian, a faery maiden. The faeries were present in the king's company and they were abroad in the island of Britain during his reign:

---

[92] Holinshed, *Chronicles*, Book V, c.14; Lydgate, *The Fall of Princes*, 1431-8, Book VIII, c.24

"In days of old, when Arthur fill'd the throne…
The king of elves and tiny fairy queen
Gambolled on heaths and danced on every green."[93]

Arthur became clearly integrated into the faery heritage of the British Isles.  What's more, in returning to the earlier point about the place of his burial, or concealment, he was also absorbed into Britain's faery geography.

Arthur still sleeps, awaiting the call to save this land, and many of the places where he and his knights are believed to be slumbering are exactly the kinds of site that we have already seen to be associated with the faery population. Victorian poet Philip James Bailey underlined this in his epic *A Spiritual Legend.*  He described "fairy Avalon, still where Arthur rules" over a land of ancient monuments, "With cromlech crowned, gray cairn, or fairy knoll/ Or lithic dance of giants 'neath the moon."[94]  Many prehistoric sites have Arthurian links: for example, Castle-an-Dinas hillfort and Arthur's Hall on Bodmin Moor in Cornwall, the chamber tomb of Arthur's Stone in Herefordshire, another such on Cefn Bryn in Gower, or the henge outside Penrith that's known as King Arthur's Round Table.  However, the ones that concern us now are those where Arthur might be still present, patiently awaiting the call.[95]

At Cadbury Castle in Somerset there is an impressive hillfort renowned to this day as the site of Camelot.  Arthur's Well is found nearby and Arthur's causeway leads from there to Glastonbury.  Most importantly, though, the hill is hollow, and the king and his knights sit within behind golden gates.  Once a year, on Midsummer's Eve, this portal opens and it is possible to see inside.  Otherwise, every full moon, Arthur and

---

[93] John Dryden, 'Chaucer's *The Wife of Bath- Her Tale*;' see too Thomas Parnell, *A Fairy Tale in the Ancient English Style.*
[94] In *The Mystic, and other poems*, 1855.
[95] See too Ithell Colquhoun, *The Living Stones,* 'Traces of King Arthur.'

his men ride out to circle the hill and water their horses at the well.

At Sewingshields in Northumberland, under the ruins of the medieval castle, a hall was once discovered by a local farmer where armed men and hunting hounds slept around a roaring, fuel-less fire.  The farmer began to unsheathe a sword and this caused the warriors to start to stir and wake up.  The man fled in terror- and could never find his way in again.  Very similar stories are attached to Richmond Castle in North Yorkshire and, also in Northumberland, to Brinkburn Priory and to Dunstanburgh on the coast.

Arthur is also believed to sleep elsewhere in England: beneath either St Catherine's Hill in Hampshire or Alderley Edge in Cheshire, under Freebrough Hill near Whitby, in a cave at The Sneep on the River Derwent in County Durham, and at three sites in Cumberland: at Ravenglass Roman Fort, under Threlkeld Fall near Keswick and below the peak of Blencathra. He might also be found under Arthur's Seat, outside Edinburgh, and in Wales at Caerleon, Craig-y-Ddinas, Ogo'r Dinas, Pumsaint near Lampeter and, lastly, on the slopes of Snowdon.

In fact, it isn't always Arthur who is associated with these 'sleeping hero' stories.  At Dunstanburgh castle the individual is named as 'Guy the Seeker.'  On the Eildon Hills in Roxburghshire, a hill known as the Lucken Hare is the place where a man who sold horses to the local faeries was taken underground to be shown some sleeping knights and their steeds.  He was led there by an old man who turned out to be none other than the famous Thomas of Erceldoune, or Thomas the Rhymer, the man who had met the faery queen on the hills and had travelled with her into Faery.  In this particular story, the horse dealer was told that whoever drew a sword and blew on a horn lying on a table would be king of Britain- provided that he chose correctly which of the two items to pick up first.  The unlucky horse dealer chose the horn first- and was swept out of the subterranean hall by a faery whirlwind.

Thomas of Erceldoune is also reputed to be living with the faeries and occasionally buying horses for the slumbering knights beneath Dumbarton Rock on the Clyde as well as under the yew-capped *sithean* at Tomnahurich.  What's fascinating about these particular accounts is the fact that it's a mortal man who has ventured into the faeryland who has now become the enchanted guardian of the undying human king and his retinue.  They are all enveloped in an immortal glamour and cannot perish until their missions are fulfilled.

In the wider context of this book, we see that these accounts represent another aspect of the enchantment of the land. Here, rather than the faeries themselves, it is their mortal collaborators or companions who are involved, but the underlying motivation is the same: it is to connect the fabric of the islands with the deepest motifs of our mythology.  The features of the landscape are tied in to the core themes of our legends, so that the mortal inhabitants of Britain are not alone, but are continually sustained by a profound connections to our past.

## The Soul of the Land

The faery folk have been present in Britain for untold generations.  The evidence of place names and tradition demonstrate their ancient links to monuments, places and plants and show how deeply embedded they are in our landscape.  None know the land- its features, climate and resources- better than they.  Artists have rightly called them the *genii loci* or spirits of place, the soul of the island of Britain.

In past centuries, the human population was more intimately connected to its environment and more keenly aware of the supernatural presence alongside which they lived.  In modern times, most of us have lost that closeness and that consciousness; it is most often artists and poets who possess the sensibility and perceptiveness to detect the continuing proximity of the faeries and their true role of the essential spirits of this land.

Doubtless, being open to these sensations is important; an individual may need to have a certain mindset in the first place. Over and above that, though, I think the 'spirit of place' I've been trying to define in this book, amounts to this: the Britishness of British faeries in large measure derives from a sense of depth of time and connection. Whatever the nature of the initial experience(s) that linked a faery or elf or brownie to a particular site, what instils a tangible- if elusive- meaning is the body of accrued associations that have accumulated over subsequent centuries. These create a weight of significance, a resonance across generations, that has meaning and magic in itself (the story) as well as bestowing the sensation of connecting with previous believers. Over centuries, believers have responded to and shaped the landscape in light of its supernatural links and connotations- "This happened here to your predecessor."

What feels meaningful, therefore, is the awareness of the deep roots of the faery tradition, coupled with the consciousness that it is an inheritance- a shared perception passed down over ages of the interaction between place, incident and emotion.

I suspect that I'm still struggling to express adequately the combined power of landscape, meaning and myth, as it strikes me as a feeling, not a theory, that's generated by certain locations. To understand my response, it helps for me to set faerylore alongside other national accounts, such as the 'Matter of Britain' (the Arthurian stories) and the legends of the *Mabinogion*. What these all evoke for me is a sense of profound mystery- and romance; there's an elusive contact with something very ancient, the meaning of which I haven't yet wholly grasped. That- intangible and vague as it may sound- is the inspiration that ultimately underlies this book.